YOUTH SPECIALTIES TITLES

Professional Resources
Developing Spiritual Growth in Junior High Students
Equipped to Serve
Help! I'm a Volunteer Youth Worker!
Help! I'm a Sunday School Teacher!
How to Recruit and Train Volunteer Youth Workers
    (previously released as Unsung Heroes)
The Ministry of Nurture
One Kid at a Time
Peer Counseling in Youth Groups
Advanced Peer Counseling in Youth Groups

Discussion Starter Resources
Get 'Em Talking
High School TalkSheets
Junior High TalkSheets
High School TalkSheets: Psalms and Proverbs
Junior High TalkSheets: Psalms and Proverbs
More High School TalkSheets
More Junior High TalkSheets
Parent Ministry TalkSheets
Would You Rather . . . ?

Ideas Library
Ideas Combo 1-4, 5-8, 9-12, 13-16, 17-20, 21-24, 25-28,
    29-32, 33-36, 37-40, 41-44, 45-48, 49-52, 53, 54
Ideas Index

Youth Ministry Programming
Compassionate Kids
Creative Bible Lessons on the Life of Christ
Creative Programming Ideas for Junior High Ministry
Creative Socials and Special Events
Dramatic Pauses
Facing Your Future
Great Fundraising Ideas for Youth Groups
Great Ideas for Small Youth Groups
Great Retreats for Youth Groups
Greatest Skits on Earth
Greatest Skits on Earth, Volume 2
Holiday Ideas for Youth Groups (Revised Edition)
Hot Illustrations for Youth Talks
Hot Talks
Junior High Game Nights
More Junior High Game Nights
Play It! Great Games for Groups
Play It Again! More Great Games for Groups
Road Trip

Super Sketches for Youth Ministry
Teaching the Bible Creatively
Up Close and Personal: How to Build Community
in Your Youth Group

4th-6th Grade Ministry
Attention Grabbers for 4th-6th Graders
4th-6th Grade TalkSheets
Great Games for 4th-6th Graders
How to Survive Middle School
Incredible Stories
More Attention Grabbers for 4th-6th Graders
More Great Games for 4th-6th Graders
Quick and Easy Activities for 4th-6th Graders
More Quick and Easy Activities for 4th-6th Graders
Teach 'Toons

Clip Art
ArtSource Volume 1—Fantastic Activities
ArtSource Volume 2—Borders, Symbols, Holidays,
and Attention Getters
ArtSource Volume 3—Sports
ArtSource Volume 4—Phrases and Verses
ArtSource Volume 5—Amazing Oddities and Appalling Images
ArtSource Volume 6—Spiritual Topics
ArtSource Volume 7—Variety Pack
Youth Specialties Clip Art Book
Youth Specialties Clip Art Book, Volume 2

Video
Edge TV
God Views
The Heart of Youth Ministry: A Morning with Mike Yaconelli
Next Time I Fall in Love Video Curriculum
Promo Spots for Junior High Game Nights
Resource Seminar Video Series
Understanding Your Teenager Video Curriculum
Witnesses

Student Books
Going the Distance
Grow for It Journal
Grow for It Journal through the Scriptures
How to Live with Your Parents without Losing Your Mind
I Don't Remember Dropping the Skunk, but I Do Remember Trying
to Breathe
Next Time I Fall in Love
Next Time I Fall in Love Journal
101 Things to Do During a Dull Sermon

50 Life Lessons
from the Scriptures

Mark Oestreicher

Youth
Specialties

[OUR NAME IS THE AGE]

ZondervanPublishingHouse
Grand Rapids, Michigan
A Division of *HarperCollins* Publishers

Wild Truth Journal: 50 Life Lessons from the Scriptures

Youth Specialties Books are published by Zondervan Publishing House, 5300 Patterson SE, Grand Rapids, Michigan 49530.

Edited by Noel Becchetti and Lorraine Triggs
Typography and design by Patton Brothers Design, San Diego

Printed in the United States of America

02 / ML / 17 16 15 14 13 12 11

To Liesl Maria: I hope you'll grow up to love these characters and the God who made both them and you.

Table of Contents

Acknowledgements

Thanks: Jeannie, for your support; Mom & Dad O, for your brainstorming input; Todd Temple and Noel Becchetti, for your excellent input; Derrick Riggs, Paul Syverson and Jerod Gross, for holding me accountable to God (and writing); Ben Joiner, Michael Dave, Garrett Chenault and Drew Osborne (my junior high guys discipleship group), for your encouragement and prayers.

Introduction

I'm totally pumped to introduce you to some friends. The characters you'll read about on the following pages aren't just made up. All but two of them were real live people—people with the same feelings, problems, mistakes, joys, frustrations, hurts, complaints, sins, habits, talents, attitudes, and reactions you have today! Even the two characters who weren't real were in a story Jesus told, and they might as well have been real—their lessons sure are!

My hope for you, as you spend the next few months plugging through this book, is that you'll not only learn about some of the amazing characters in the Bible, but also that you'll see how much the lessons from their lives can apply to your life. So have fun! Set aside a specific time each week to work through a couple of lessons. I'd encourage you to try two or three a week. But even one a week would be great—that way the book will last you almost a year! You'll see—studying the Bible can be interesting and fun!

Mark Oestreicher

Note to Leaders

This book was written so students can use it without any supervision. However, it will also work well in a small group setting.

Agree with your students on a set number of lessons they'll do per week. Then hold them to that agreement. Call your students during the week and encourage them. If the number of lessons turns out to be too big or too small—change it! Just make sure the whole group stays at the same place in the book, or your discussions will be impaired.

Set a time, once a week, to get together with your group of students and discuss the lessons they completed the previous week (complete the lessons yourself as well). You might find it's fun to have the students lead each other (and you) through the lessons.

This book was written with a couple of goals in mind. I wanted to make sure that students actually had to interact with the Bible. Each lesson forces students to look up a passage, read it, and answer questions about the content. Hopefully, this exercise will encourage and train students to stay in the Word long after this book is filled out and forgotten.

The second goal was to directly apply the point of each lesson to students' lives. That's on the second page of each lesson. Most lessons call for "this week I'll do …" answers. Be sure to follow up on these with your students.

I'm excited you've chosen **Wild Truth Journal** to study with your students. I know God will honor your efforts!

Kid King JOEY

Real Name: _____

King JOEY became the King when he was just a kid! He
wanted to serve God, but didn't know what to do because
the only copy of the Book of the Law (his Bible) was lost.
When it was found, he had a big decision to make!

Flashback

(Whenever you read about a Bible character, fill in his
or her real name at the top of each new page.)

Read II Kings 22:1-2; 23:1-3; 25

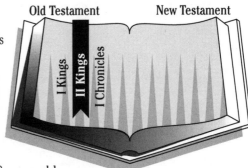

Old Testament   New Testament

I Kings   II Kings   I Chronicles

● ● ● ● ● ● ● ● ● ●

When did JOEY become king?

❏ 2 months old   ❏ 8 years old
❏ 2 years old   ❏ 13 years old

Which ways didn't JOEY turn (verse 2, check all that apply)?

❏ right   ❏ left   ❏ in
❏ up   ❏ down   ❏ diagonally

What did King JOEY do in chapter 23, verses 1-3?

Where did he do it?

❏ in school   ❏ in front of the temple
❏ in a laundromat   ❏ in Paris

How did the people respond to JOEY's actions?

FAST FORWARD

King JOEY had great influence over the Jewish people.

Whom do you have the power to influence?

Tell about a time you influenced someone negatively:

Tell about a time you influenced someone positively:

What's one thing you could do this week to influence someone you know in a positive way? (Be specific.)

Whom you'll influence	What you'll do	When you'll do it

Stuck Up UZZIE

Real Name:

UZZIE was a cool king—for a while. He lived for God and had lots of success. But then things took a bad turn, and he spent the rest of his life isolated, covered with leprosy.

 Flashback

Read 2 Chronicles 26:3-5, 16-23

● ● ● ● ● ● ● ● ●

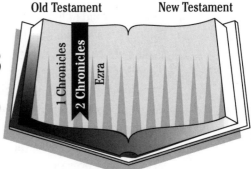

Old Testament   New Testament

1 Chronicles | 2 Chronicles | Ezra

UZZIE was successful as long as he . . .
- ❏ ate his Wheaties
- ❏ sought the Lord
- ❏ always made his bed
- ❏ wore his lucky shoes

What sin led to UZZIE's downfall? (Hint: it's in verse 16.)

What did UZZIE burn on the altar?
- ❏ toast
- ❏ a chicken dinner
- ❏ his hand
- ❏ incense

Why was this incense thing a big deal?

FAST FORWARD

When is pride healthy?

When is pride harmful?

Check a box for each situation to show if you think it's healthy pride or harmful pride:

Healthy   Harmful

❏   ❏   Teresa is proud of her mother, who just finished college after eight years of night school.

❏   ❏   Philip got a silver medal at the swim meet last week and wore it to school every day to make sure everyone knew.

❏   ❏   Danielle got an A on her math test, and ran home to tell her mom.

❏   ❏   Tim's baseball team took second place in their league. He got a small trophy, which he keeps on his shelf in his room.

❏   ❏   Terence was so confident of his basketball skills that he told his teammates to pass the ball to him every chance they got.

❏   ❏   Jill is a babe—everyone knows it, including her. She uses her good looks to get what she wants.

If someone were to say you were too proud about something, what would it be?

Rank these solutions to pride from 1 (great solution) to 6 (lousy solution):

____ realize God gave me everything, including the thing I'm proud of

____ don't promote myself—don't point out my skills or best features to everyone

____ don't brag

____ whip myself with a bamboo stick

____ use my skill, ability, or feature for good

____ give myself small electric shocks every time I brag

Now go back and circle one solution you'll put into practice this week.

LAZ, The Dead Guy

Real Name: _____

LAZ was one of Jesus' best friends. One day he caught a little cold, and one thing led to another. Before he could say "Call the doctor," he wasn't able to talk!

 Flashback

Read John 11:17-44
(so it's a little long, don't be a wimp!)

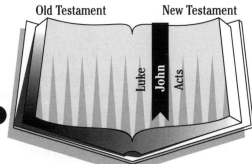

Old Testament   New Testament

Luke   John   Acts

● ● ● ● ● ● ● ●

LAZ spent the last four days hanging out:
- ❏ at a bar
- ❏ in a cave
- ❏ at a video arcade
- ❏ in the temple
- ❏ at the beach

*LAZ had a **major** problem! What was it? (Check all that apply, and then circle the biggest problem.)*
- ❏ he'd lost his appetite
- ❏ he was having body odor problems
- ❏ he was wearing clothes that didn't allow much movement
- ❏ he was dead
- ❏ his sisters wouldn't talk to him
- ❏ everyone around him was crying all the time

How did Jesus fix LAZ's problem?

Why did Jesus fix LAZ's problem?

FAST FORWARD

List four problems that are common for students your age:

Circle the two that are problems for you.

There are lots of different ways Jesus could fix your problem. List three different things Jesus could do to help:

Dear God,

Write a prayer to God, asking for help with your problem.

Love,

MOE'S BRO

Real Name: [   ]

MOE'S BRO had a good deal going! He was playing a major role in leading the people of Israel. But he made a bad choice the size of King Kong!

 Flashback

Read Exodus 32:1-8, 19-25

Old Testament   New Testament

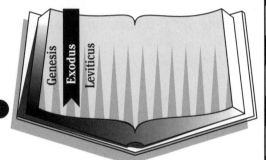

Genesis   Exodus   Leviticus

● ● ● ● ● ● ● ●

Describe MOE'S BRO's sin:

Where was Moses during all this?
- ❏ out shopping
- ❏ on the mountain
- ❏ on a speaking tour
- ❏ offering sacrifices

What shape was the idol?
- ❏ a calf
- ❏ a lion
- ❏ the Empire State Building
- ❏ a hamster

When Moses asked his brother why he made the idol, MOE'S BRO made the sin worse! How?

FAST FORWARD

Check the statement that most applies to you:

____ I sin sometimes.
____ I never sin, but I'm a huge liar.

Name five sins common for students your age:

What's the best thing to do when you sin? (Check all that are true.)

____ run and hide
____ admit my sin to God and anyone else involved
____ start hitting someone
____ lie to cover it up
____ ask for forgiveness from God and anyone who was hurt by my sin
____ feel really guilty about it forever
____ learn from my sin

Think and pray. First, confess some recent sins to God. Then, think about what you can learn or what you need to do to fix any wrongs. Check here when you carried out your plans: ☐

WEATHER MAN

Real Name:

You probably know a lot about this guy. He was, and is, after all, kind of central to Christianity! But what he did in this story is truly remarkable. And the fact that he can do the same in your life is even more remarkable!

 Flashback

Read Mark 4:35-41

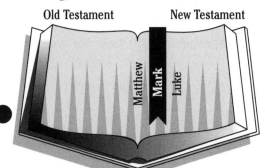

Old Testament   New Testament

Matthew Mark Luke

● ● ● ● ● ● ● ●

Where were WEATHER MAN and his friends?
- ❏ on a train in a tunnel
- ❏ on a camel in the desert
- ❏ in a boat on a lake
- ❏ in a restaurant on the boulevard

What was WEATHER MAN doing while his friends were freaking out?
- ❏ fishing
- ❏ preaching
- ❏ shucking oysters
- ❏ working out
- ❏ sleeping

What did he do?

Choose a title for a movie based on this story:
- ❏ Water Water Everywhere
- ❏ Down by the Sea
- ❏ Stop Waving!
- ❏ Waterworld
- ❏ Shut Up!

FAST FORWARD

Jenna's parents just told her they're going to get a divorce. She's really scared and torn up inside. To make things worse, the boy she likes at school made it obvious today that he isn't interested in her at all. To top it off, her science teacher told her, "If you don't start doing better, I'll have to meet with your parents."

What could WEATHER MAN do for Jenna?

Check some of the "storms" you've experienced:

____ bad grades	____ being really sick
____ teacher doesn't like me	____ not making a sports team
____ friend ignores me	____ parents' fighting
____ parents' divorce	____ moved to a new city or school
____ don't have friends	____ teased or mocked by kids at school
____ feeling like God isn't there	____ lost something special
____ friend spreads rumor about me	____ felt like I wasn't good enough
____ parent yells at me	____ did something really stupid
____ tempted to do something bad	____ other:
____ relative or friend dying	

Circle one of the "storms" above that you're dealing with now.

Write a prayer to WEATHER MAN, asking him to help you with that "storm."

Dear WEATHER MAN,

Love,

NEZZY,
King of the Beasts

Real Name:

NEZZY was an OK king some of the time. But he was a bit too convinced that he was the coolest guy around. God had an interesting way of taking **NEZZY** down a few notches.

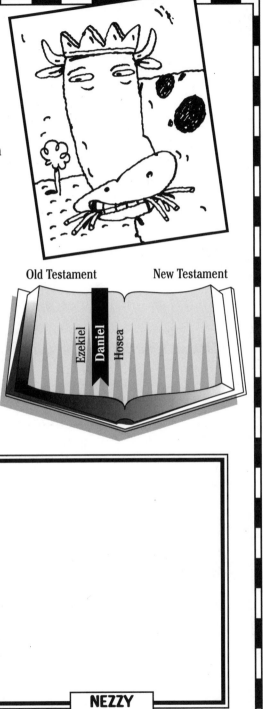

Flashback

Read Daniel 4:28-37

Old Testament   New Testament

Ezekiel Daniel Hosea

What happened to NEZZY? Why?

How did he react?

What happened next?

Draw a picture of NEZZY while he was a wild child (look in verse 33):

NEZZY

FAST FORWARD

Name a TV or movie actor who you believe thinks too highly of him or herself:

How do people act when they think too highly of themselves?

Place an X on the line that matches your view of yourself:

/————————————/————————————/————————————/

1. I think I'm scum

2. I think less of myself than I should

3. I think more highly of myself than I should

4. I am perfect

How do you find the balance between being stuck up and always being down on yourself?

SKiPPER,
the Dryland Boat Builder

Real Name: _____

God asked **SKiPPER** to do something that seemed really strange. And the amazing thing is that we see no sign of **SKiPPER** hesitating at all—he just did it! People made fun of him, teased him, and called him a crazy old man. But he went ahead and did what God asked him to do. And was he ever glad he did!

Flashback

Read Genesis 6:9-22

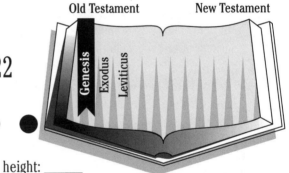

Old Testament   New Testament

Genesis   Exodus   Leviticus

● ● ● ● ● ● ● ●

What were the dimensions of the boat?

length: _____   width: _____   height: _____

This is a Crazy Meter. Draw in a needle to show just how crazy this job must've seemed to SKIPPER when God first asked him to do it:

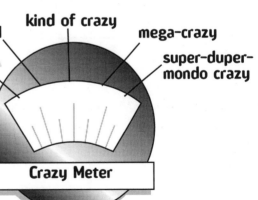

a little weird   kind of crazy   mega-crazy

totally normal   super-duper-mondo crazy

Crazy Meter

Why did SKIPPER build the boat?

FAST FORWARD

Here are some crazy things you could do for God.
Check three that you would like to try:

____ help my brother or sister with his or her chores
____ eat lunch with a loner at school
____ volunteer at a local soup kitchen
____ do what my parents say, even when it doesn't seem fair
____ share my faith with someone at school
____ say only good things about others
____ ask my friends to stop swearing around me
____ start a Bible study or prayer group at school
____ memorize one new Bible verse each week
____ other:_____

Choose one of the three things you checked off and write a plan for
how you will do it.

My "crazy" act for God	How I'm going to do it	When I'm going to do it

Prove it to Me
TOM

Real Name:

TOM wasn't there. He didn't see what happened. Everyone else was there and saw what happened. And they expected him to believe them. **TOM** was having a pretty hard time believing what he didn't see himself!

Flashback

Read John 20:24-31

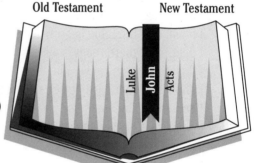

Old Testament   New Testament

Luke   John   Acts

● ● ● ● ● ● ● ● ●

TOM's job was:
- ❑ prophet
- ❑ king of Israel
- ❑ disciple of Jesus
- ❑ used car salesman

TOM's problem was:

What proof did TOM ask for?
- ❑ Jesus' driver's license
- ❑ a note from Jesus' mom
- ❑ to touch the nail holes
- ❑ to see Jesus for himself

How did Jesus deal with TOM's problem?

FAST FORWARD

Rank the following doubts from 1 to 10
(10 = one of my biggest doubts; 1 = I don't doubt this at all)

___ I doubt that God really cares about me
___ I doubt that the Bible is error-free
___ I doubt that God exists
___ I doubt that Jesus was raised from the dead
___ I doubt that the Bible has anything to say to me
___ I doubt that there really is a hell
___ I doubt that Jesus never sinned
___ I doubt that there are demons and angels
___ I doubt that God hears my prayers
___ I doubt that Mary (Jesus' mom) was a virgin

True or False:

T   **F**   I'm a bad Christian if I have doubts

If Jesus helped TOM deal with his doubts, how could he help you with yours?

Hard Knocks PABLO

Real Name: [   ]

We know a ton about PABLO, probably more than almost any other Bible character except Jesus. But in this lesson we're going to focus on one aspect of his life:

(To find out what it is, solve the puzzle by moving back two letters in the alphabet.)

$\overline{\text{V}}$ $\overline{\text{Q}}$ $\overline{\text{W}}$ $\overline{\text{I}}$ $\overline{\text{J}}$ $\overline{\text{V}}$ $\overline{\text{K}}$ $\overline{\text{O}}$ $\overline{\text{G}}$ $\overline{\text{U}}$

Flashback

Read 2 Corinthians 11:24-27

● ● ● ● ● ● ● ● ●

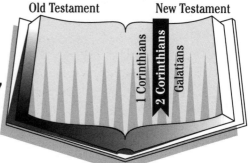

Old Testament / New Testament
1 Corinthians / 2 Corinthians / Galatians

PABLO's plights were (check all that apply):

- ❏ whipping
- ❏ caught in blizzard
- ❏ old lady next door yelling at him
- ❏ beatings
- ❏ thirst
- ❏ lack of sleep
- ❏ naked
- ❏ plane crash
- ❏ danger from non-Jews

- ❏ stoning
- ❏ shipwrecked
- ❏ lost at sea
- ❏ hunger
- ❏ ran out of diet cola
- ❏ cold
- ❏ clothing horribly out of style
- ❏ danger from Jews
- ❏ danger from the Jetsons

Circle the situations above that would be the worst for you.

FAST FORWARD

Add to the list seven more tough times that students your age have:

1. parents' divorce
2. friends treat you bad
3. school stress
4.
5.
6.
7.
8.
9.
10.

What's the most difficult thing that's ever happened to you?

How did you handle it?

Why do you think God allows difficult times in our lives?

Write a prayer to God, asking for help with a difficult situation, or for a friend who is struggling with a difficult situation:

Dear GOD,

Love,

MOE: Mr. Excuses

Real Name: _____

MOE's life and leadership of God's people cover a big chunk of the Old Testament. God used him in some great ways over lots of years. But **MOE**'s reaction, when God first asked him to take the leadership job, wasn't quite what you might expect.

Flashback

Read Exodus 3:1-5, 10-16; 4:1-13

● ● ● ● ● ● ● ●

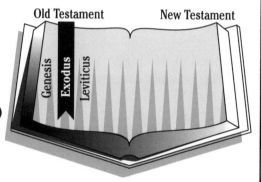

Circle MOE's response to what God told him:

He was excited

He cried and ran away

He got right down to business

He made excuses why God couldn't use him

He hired someone else to do the job

Check five excuses MOE used:

____ I'm too old
____ They won't listen to me
____ I'm not smart enough
____ They won't know who God is
____ I don't want to do it
____ Why?

____ I'm too short
____ I'm a nobody
____ Please send someone else
____ I don't feel like it
____ I don't speak well
____ How much does it pay?

FAST FORWARD

Place an X on the line that best describes your feelings about this statement:

"God can use me to do some amazing things."

/————————————/————————————/————————————/
1. Not a chance!   **2.** Not likely   **3.** I guess so   **4.** You bet!

What reasons come to mind when you think God can't use you?

___ I don't speak well
___ People will make fun of me
___ I'm too young
___ I don't have time
___ I'm not popular enough

___ I'm too shy
___ I'm not smart enough
___ I'm not good-looking enough
___ I'm afraid to stick out

Choose the top three excuses from the list above you might use if God asked you to do something huge.

Write one way God could use you this week:

WISE GUY, the
King of Good Decisions

Real Name:

When God told this king he could have anything he wanted, he asked for wisdom. He got it! Check out this really cool decision.

 Flashback

Read 1 Kings 3:16-28

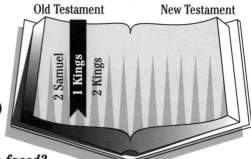

Old Testament   New Testament

2 Samuel 1 Kings 2 Kings

What was WISE GUY's solution to the problem he faced?

❏ chop the baby in half
❏ have the mothers offer sacrifices to God
❏ send the women to jail
❏ schedule a DNA test

Assuming you wouldn't have thought of the creative way WISE GUY answered, what decision would you have made if you were on his throne?

If you were WISE GUY, and God said you could have anything you wanted, what would you ask for?

FAST FORWARD

Making good decisions is a big part of life. Give advice to these three students who are having a difficult time knowing what to do.

1. **Claudia**, Teresa, and Kim have been best friends — but Teresa and Kim are in a major fight. Both girls have told Claudia that she can only be friends with one of them.

2. **Alex** knows that Peter copied off his test. It really makes him mad! But Peter is, like, the most popular kid in the entire school. If Alex says anything, he'll never be popular.

3. **Jenny's** parents are out of town for the night. She is staying with a new friend from school—Tonya. After Jenny is at Tonya's for a couple hours, other people start coming over. Before long it's a big-time party with lots of drinking, smoking, and making out.

List two or three hard decisions you've had to make in the last year.

A hard decision I have to make now or soon is:

Give yourself some advice:

JON,
the Friend of Friends

Real Name:

Aren't good friends great to have? It's not very often we can find really good friends—friends we can trust. **JON** was a friend worth keeping—a friend for life!

 Flashback

Read 1 Samuel 20:1-17

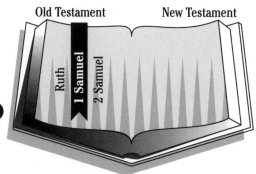

Old Testament   New Testament

Ruth   1 Samuel   2 Samuel

● ● ● ● ● ● ● ● ●

JON's best friend was:

❑ Barney
❑ Jeff
❑ Saul

❑ David
❑ Mickey Mouse
❑ that guy from the *Ernest* movies

What are some of the reasons JON and his friend were such good buddies? What about their friendship made it good (check all that apply)?

❑ loyalty
❑ honesty
❑ they defended each other
❑ they played together on
  the Jerusalem soccer club

❑ love for each other
❑ they had the same homeroom
❑ concern for each other's safety
❑ they both liked Sega

FAST FORWARD

Friend Rater. Put your pen or pencil on box #1. Then, move it down the correct path to indicate a "yes" or "no" answer to question #1. Do the same for question #2, #3, and so on. This will give you an idea of how good a friend you are.

```
                    #1
                 YES    NO
              #2          #2
           YES   NO    YES   NO
         #3        #3        #3
      YES  NO   YES   NO  YES   NO
     #4       #4        #4        #4
   YES NO  YES  NO  YES   NO  YES  NO
  #5     #5      #5      #5      #5
 YES NO YES NO YES NO YES NO YES NO
```

| Awesome Friend | Great Friend | Good Friend | So-so Friend | Wimpy Friend | Lousy Friend |

1. I am trustworthy. My friends can always trust me.

2. I am loyal. My friends know I'll always be there for them.

3. I am honest. I tell the truth to my friends and about my friends.

4. I am an encourager. I'm always building my friends up, not tearing them down.

5. I am giving. I regularly try to meet my friends' needs.

My best friendship quality is . . .

The friendship quality I need to work on the most is . . .

One way I can improve as a friend this week is . . .

I will practice this friendship improvement with (name someone) . . .

I will do this (name a time) . . .

KING #1—
the Mad Monarch

Real Name:

This guy was Israel's first king, and he seemed to want to serve God at first. But as the years went by, his loyalty to God got shaky. One day he'd try to live for God, and the next day he'd be worshipping some false god or idol. Near the end of his life, there was one issue that tripped him up over and over again.

Read 1 Samuel 18:5-16

Old Testament   New Testament

Ruth   1 Samuel   2 Samuel

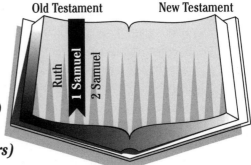

● ● ● ● ● ● ● ●

KING #1's problem was. . . (unscramble the letters)

O S A L U J E Y _____

Why was KING #1 this way?

What did he do about it?

If the song in verse 7 were sung today, which musician or group would do it best?

FAST FORWARD

Write about a time when you felt jealous.

Check the three things that would make you the most jealous:

____ someone who gets better grades but with less effort than I

____ someone prettier or more handsome than I

____ someone more popular than I

____ someone who has more money than I

____ someone who always gets his or her way

____ someone who wears better clothes than I

____ someone whose parents let him or her do anything

____ someone who is a better athlete than I

____ someone with a totally hot boyfriend or girlfriend

____ someone taller than I

____ someone thinner than I

____ someone with more artistic ability than I

____ someone always chosen for things I want to do

Someone I'm jealous of now is:

Why?

List some reasons why your jealousy of this person only makes things worse.

HAMMERHEAD,
the Nap Time Monitor

Real Name: _____

OK, take a seat and brace yourself. You've probably never heard of this gutsy lady. And it's a totally cool story! **HAMMERHEAD** and her people were camped out near a battle. One of the enemy leaders escapes and shows up at her tent. That's where we pick up.

Flashback

Read Judges 4:17-22

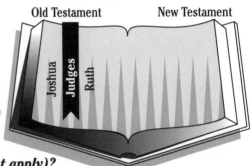

Old Testament   New Testament

Joshua **Judges** Ruth

● ● ● ● ● ● ● ● ●

What did Hammerhead do for Sisera (check all that apply)?

❑ gave him milk
❑ relieved his tension headache

❑ covered him up
❑ fed him dinner

If Hammerhead's story were made into a movie, what would you call it? Whom would you get to play her part?

Do you think you could've done what Hammerhead did? Why or why not?

FAST FORWARD

What would you do in these difficult situations:

1. Your English teacher makes fun of Christians all the time. She always says they're nonthinkers and "mindless." She knows you're a Christian, and today, during one of her moods, she asks you to come to the front of the class and tell everyone why you believe in God.
What do you do? What do you say?

2. You can't believe it! Your two closest friends just told you that they tried a joint in the bathroom! And now the assistant principal is standing in front of your class saying, "Anyone who knows anything about someone smoking marijuana in the bathroom should come to my office at the next break."
What do you do? What do you say?

How could God help you in these situations?

*What are a few difficult things that you've had to do
(or that a friend has had to do)?*

How could God have helped you in one of these (or how did he help)?

ANDY & SOPHiE,
the King and Queen of Lies

Real Names:

The Christians in the early church did something cool—people who had more money than others occasionally sold land and gave the money to the church. The money then was given to people in the church who needed it. **ANDY** and **SOPHiE** did this, but they pulled a fast one along the way—and faced huge consequences as a result!

 Flashback

Read Acts 4:32—5:11

● ● ● ● ● ● ● ● ● ●

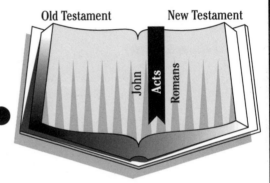

Old Testament   New Testament

John Acts Romans

True or False:

T F ANDY & SOPHIE sold some land in order to give money to the church
T F ANDY & SOPHIE gave a bunch of money to the church
T F ANDY & SOPHIE gave all the money to the church
T F ANDY & SOPHIE got in trouble because they didn't give all the money to the church
T F ANDY & SOPHIE lied about how much they were giving
T F The consequences of ANDY & SOPHIE's lie was that they had to clean the church bathrooms for a month
T F ANDY & SOPHIE never told another lie

(In case you didn't catch it, they didn't get into trouble because of the size of their gift. They got in trouble because they lied!)

__What would your reaction have been if you'd been standing nearby, watching all this?__

FAST FORWARD

What's wrong with lying?

What are some of the consequences of lying?

Why do people lie?

What's the biggest lie you've ever told?

What's the last lie you told? (Be honest.)

What would happen if you went back and told the truth?

No Go JOE

Real Name: [   ]

The boss' wife is a total babe. She decides her husband is not quite the hunk that **JOE** is, and makes her desires clear to him. Is she a temptation for **JOE**? You bet! If she wasn't a temptation, he wouldn't have reacted the way he did. Check it out.

 Flashback

Read Genesis 39:1-12

● ● ● ● ● ● ● ● ●

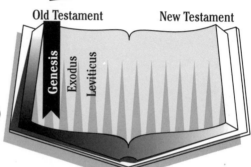

JOE's job was:

❏ fry cook
❏ business manager

❏ pyramid builder
❏ cloak salesman

If Hollywood made a movie of this story, who would play JOE? Who would play the woman in the story?

Which of these would you choose as the title of the movie?

____ Leave Me Alone   ____ Tempting the Cloak off My Back   ____ Run, JOE, Run

____ Sex with the Boss' Wife? Uh-uh!   ____ Tempt Me Like You Know Me

Why do you think JOE reacted the way he did?

FAST FORWARD

List ten temptations students your age face.
(Remember—some are temptations to *do* certain things, others could be temptations <u>not</u> to do certain things.)

1.
2.
3.
4.
5.
6.
7.
8.
9.
10.

Now go back and circle the top three temptations you face.

Temptation Counterattack

The Attack: What's a temptation you face regularly?

Counterattack Plan: What can you do this week to overcome this temptation, with God's help?

DONKEY BOY,
the Red-Faced Rider

Real Name: _____

Whoa! What a trippy story! Poor donkey! **DONKEY BOY** got embarrassed in front of his servants because it looked like he didn't know how to control his animal.

 Flashback

Read Numbers 22:21-33

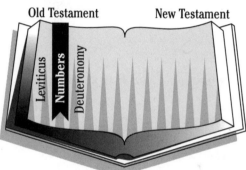

● ● ● ● ● ● ● ●

What did the donkey see?

❑ a ghost
❑ a cute burro
❑ a bully donkey from school

❑ an angel
❑ a glue factory

How did DONKEY BOY react to the embarrassing situation?

How did the donkey react to DONKEY BOY?

What would you have said if you were the donkey?

FAST FORWARD

Describe a really embarrassing situation that happened to you:

How did you respond to your embarrassing situation?

How would you rate your response?

/——————————/——————————/——————————/

Way bad　　　　**Not good**　　　　**OK**　　　　**Good**

What, if anything, would have been a better response?

How will you try to respond the next time you get embarrassed?

LiTTLE TiMMY,
the Teenage Teacher

Real Name: [_____]

LiTTLE TiMMY was doing God's work in the early church. But sometimes he felt like a munchkin—too young, too small, and too unimportant to really make a difference. A guy named Paul wrote a letter to him, giving him instruction on a bunch of stuff, including how he should think about his young age.

 **Flashback**

Read 1 Timothy 4:11-16

● ● ● ● ● ● ● ● ● ●

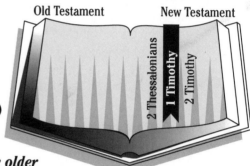

Paul told LITTLE TIMMY to be an example to the older Christians in five areas. They were:

____ hairstyle
____ love
____ speech
____ faith
____ height
____ power

____ humility
____ purity
____ life
____ strength
____ clothes
____ muscles

How was LITTLE TIMMY supposed to make sure he was an example (look at verses 15 and 16)? Check all the correct answers.

____ be diligent
____ devote himself to Scripture
____ don't play with bad boys
____ watch his life and doctrine

____ brush his teeth regularly
____ persevere
____ go to church a lot

FAST FORWARD

Next to the following "being used by God" statements, write the age at which you could do that thing:

___ be a missionary
___ tell friends about God
___ talk to a lonely person
___ pray for people with needs
___ help in the nursery at church
___ take a stand for truth
___ share a Bible verse with someone who needs encouragement
___ pray for people around the world

What would Paul write to you about what you could do right now for God and others?

Your faith is an example to your peers. But it can be an example to grown-ups, too. Pick an adult in your life whom you could be an example to. Then write down what you can do this week to be that example.

adult	what i can do	when i'll do it

NiCK at Nite

Real Name: [   ]

Pretend you live in Jesus' time. What do you do when you've got questions for Jesus, but your friends think Jesus is someone to be feared and hated? That's the problem **NiCK** had.

 Flashback

Read John 3:1-21

● ● ● ● ● ● ● ● ● ●

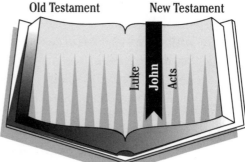

Old Testament   New Testament

Luke John Acts

NICK's friends were the . . .
- ❏ Sadducees
- ❏ Pharisees
- ❏ Jaycees
- ❏ bumblebees
- ❏ wannabes

What was NICK's real question?
- ❏ Are you God?
- ❏ Who does your hair?
- ❏ Where'd you get those cool sandals?
- ❏ What was with that HAMMERHEAD babe?

How did Jesus answer NICK's questions?

Part of Jesus' reply has become one of the most famous verses in the Bible. What is it?

John 3:_____

FAST FORWARD

Order the following questions from 1 to 10 (1=most important, 10=least important) that you'd like to ask God:

____ Why do you allow people to starve?
____ Why did my parents, or my friend's parents, divorce?
____ Why aren't I more popular?
____ Do you really care about my problems?
____ What's heaven going to be like?
____ Why did you allow that "one thing" to happen to me?
____ What do you want me to do with my life?
____ Do you really hear all my prayers?
____ Why don't you just make everyone a Christian?
____ Did Adam have a belly button?

True or False:

T   F   God wants me to ask hard questions.

Ask God

Write down a question to God, then check all the places you're willing to look for his answer:

God, i was wondering . . .

Here's where I'm willing to look for your answer:

❏ in your Word (the Bible)   ❏ from my parents
❏ under my pillow   ❏ from circumstances
❏ from my youth leader or teacher   ❏ from my horoscope
❏ from my pastor   ❏ in my conscience
❏ from 1-900-ASK-KOOK   ❏ in prayer

MOE'S MOM,
the Cruise Director

Real Name: _____

MOE'S MOM loved her son. But the king wanted him dead. She tried everything she could think of. But in the end, she just had to trust God to take care of Moe.

S.S. LITTLE MOE

 Flashback

Read Exodus 1:22—2:10

● ● ● ● ● ● ● ●

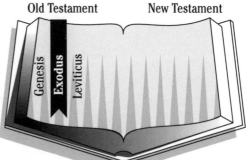

Old Testament   New Testament

Genesis | Exodus | Leviticus

Pharaoh's command was . . .
- ❏ kill all children
- ❏ kill all girls
- ❏ kill all boys
- ❏ kill all gerbils
- ❏ kill all cats named Snowball
- ❏ kill all Chia Pets

How old was Moe when he went on his first river cruise?

What did MOE'S MOM do?

Why was this such a gutsy move?

FAST FORWARD

Describe one big problem you have right now:

What can you do about it yourself?

How hard will it be for you to trust God with your problem?

```
/————————————/————————————/————————————/
1              2              3              4
mega-easy   I guess I can trust him   way hard   impossible!
```

What can you do to strengthen your trust in God this week (check all the answers you'll do this week)?

- ❏ read the Bible regularly
- ❏ talk with my youth pastor
- ❏ talk to God more often
- ❏ other:_____
- ❏ other:_____

FLAKY JAKES,
the Thankless Bunch

Real Name:

These guys had a huge problem. And they couldn't solve it themselves, no matter how hard they tried. Then Jesus came along, and in one quick move, solved their problem. How do you think they responded?

 Flashback

Read Luke 17:11-19

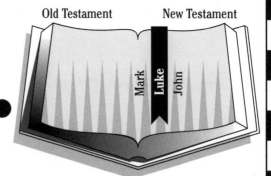

Old Testament   New Testament

Mark   Luke   John

● ● ● ● ● ● ● ● ●

Circle the correct words:
There were **(two, ten, forty-seven)** guys with **(leprosy, bad breath, dandruff, zits)** off in the distance. They **(paid, nagged, begged)** Jesus to **(heal, listen to, give money to)** them. Jesus told them to **(beg some more, shave their heads, show themselves to the priests)**. While they were doing this, **(they got hungry, they were healed, an angel appeared)**. Only one of them came back to Jesus to **(pay him, interview him, thank him, become a disciple)**.

How do you think Jesus felt when only one man returned?

If you had leprosy, and could choose which part of your body would fall off, what would you choose? Why?

FAST FORWARD

Think hard. List six things you're thankful for (not people—that's the next question!):

1.
2.
3.
4.
5.
6.   **(whew!)**

Name six people you're thankful for:

name	why I'm thankful
name	why I'm thankful
name	why I'm thankful
name	why I'm thankful
name	why I'm thankful
name	why I'm thankful

Who's one person you could thank for something this week? What will you say? When will you say this?

Person	What I'll say	When I'll say it

in Your Face NATE

Real Name:

King David had just slept with a woman who wasn't his wife, then had her husband killed so he could have her as his own wife. And King David was certainly capable of having anyone else killed who didn't like what he'd done. In walks **NATE**.

 Flashback

Read 2 Samuel 12:1-10

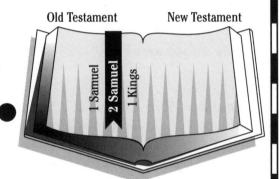

Old Testament   New Testament

1 Samuel   2 Samuel   1 Kings

● ● ● ● ● ● ● ●

How did NATE catch King David off guard?

The story NATE told was about . . .
❏ a boy named Jack and some bean seeds
❏ a boy and a girl fetching a pail of water
❏ a lamb
❏ a blonde girl and three large furry animals

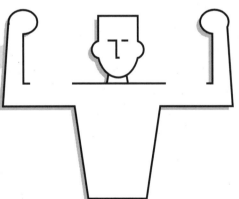

What did David say should happen to the guy in NATE's story?

Draw muscles on the picture of NATE above to represent how gutsy he was to speak the truth to David

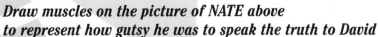

FAST FORWARD

Describe a time when you should've spoken the truth, but wimped out.

Why didn't you speak out?

Describe a time when you did speak for truth.

Why did you speak out?

Rank how hard it would be to speak out in the following "speaking the truth" situations (1=E-Z!; 10=almost impossible!).

___ Someone in your math class makes a racist remark about a new student.
___ Your friend Chris lies about a girl named Jill. Jill asks you how the lie got started.
___ You find out that your uncle cheats on his income taxes.
___ You lie to your mom and say you got an A on your science quiz. She believes you.

Is there a lie or a "wrong" in your own life that needs to be made right? What is it? What can you do this week to fix it?

The Wrong	What's Right	How I Can Make It Right

RiCHiE RiCH,
the Material Boy

Real Name: _____

Millions and millions of dollars. A huge house. Servants to do whatever you ask. This would be pretty hard to give up, wouldn't it? That's the struggle **RICHIE RICH** was facing.

 Flashback

Read Luke 18:18-23

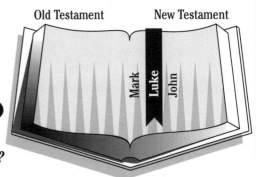

Old Testament   New Testament

Mark Luke John

● ● ● ● ● ● ● ●

What good things had RICHIE RICH done already?
(Check all the correct answers.)

❑ didn't commit adultery
❑ didn't murder
❑ didn't steal
❑ always chewed with his mouth closed

❑ didn't lie
❑ kept his socks clean
❑ gave away lots of money
❑ tried to live for God

What did Jesus ask RICHIE RICH to do?

What was RICHIE's response?

FAST FORWARD

If you had the chance to choose between going to heaven when you die or getting 500 million dollars today, which would you choose? Why?

Difficulty Thermometer:
Fill in this thermometer to
show how difficult the above
decision would be for you.

— really tough—I don't know what I'd do!

— kind of hard—they both seem pretty cool

— pretty easy—I know what I'd do

— piece of cake—easiest decision I ever made!

Name your most prized possession.

Would you give it up if . . .

. . . it meant you could continue living?	**Yes**	**No**
. . . it meant one starving kid in Africa could continue living?	**Yes**	**No**
. . . someone asked you real nice for it?	**Yes**	**No**
. . . it would prevent a handicapped kid from getting picked on?	**Yes**	**No**
. . . it somehow helped your favorite sports team win the championship?	**Yes**	**No**
. . . I traded you a candy bar?	**Yes**	**No**

Name one possession you'll give up this week.

Possession	When I'll give it up	How I'll give it up

PiG BOY,
the Short-Range Thinker

Real Name: [   ]

Growing up is tough. Sometimes it seems easier to just stay a kid. But there are so many cool things about being grown-up. Independence (making all your own decisions) is one of them. Jesus told the story of **PiG BOY** to let us know how huge God's love is for us—even when we mess up. But it's also a great picture of a young man trying to gain independence.

Flashback

Read Luke 15:11-32

● ● ● ● ● ● ● ● ●

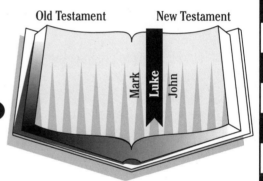

Old Testament   New Testament

Mark Luke John

What does PIG BOY ask his father for? Why?

What decision did PIG BOY make with his new-found freedom?

❏ invested money in high-risk stocks   ❏ gave all his money to the poor
❏ stayed at home and sponged off his parents ❏ spent every dime he had

What were some of the results of his decision? (Check all that are true)

❏ he wanted to eat pig slop   ❏ he made lots of moola
❏ he got the corner office with the big windows ❏ he starved
❏ he became a field worker   ❏ he got elected to government

What could PIG BOY have done with his freedom that would have been a better choice?

FAST FORWARD

What are the decisions you want to make for yourself, but you can't yet?

Circle the one decision above that you would make today if you could.

Which of the following have anything to do with gaining independence?

____ knowing how to program the VCR
____ using money
____ buying candy
____ taking care of myself
____ taking responsibity for my actions
____ doing my chores
____ owning a telescope
____ making choices for my future
____ feeding pigs
____ being really good at Super Nintendo

What's one thing you need to improve about yourself in order to gain more independence?

How can you work on this skill or character trait this week?

DEMO, the Deserter

Real Name:

Talk about being a sucker! This is the guy. If you look up "sucker" in the dictionary, it's got **DEMO**'s picture! He couldn't resist the pull of all the stuff he thought he was missing.

Flashback

Read 2 Timothy 4:9-10

● ● ● ● ● ● ● ●

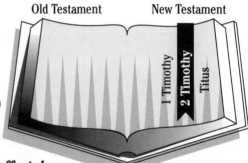

Old Testament   New Testament

1 Timothy   2 Timothy   Titus

DEMO was one of the apostle Paul's disciples.
He hung out with Paul for more than a year. What effect do
you think it would have on you if you spent all that time with Paul?

What happened to DEMO?

❏ got discovered by Hollywood   ❏ had a nasty encounter with HAMMERHEAD
❏ became a follower of another apostle   ❏ ditched Paul and went to the big city

Why did he do this?

FAST FORWARD

What are some reasons why students your age dump their relationship with God? (Check all you think are true)

- ❏ pressure from parents
- ❏ feel like they're missing out on good stuff
- ❏ don't have any Christian support
- ❏ bored in church
- ❏ can't understand the Bible
- ❏ don't "feel" close to God anymore
- ❏ boyfriends or girlfriends pulled them away
- ❏ too many rules
- ❏ afraid to share their faith but feel guilty about it
- ❏ see too many adult Christians who are hypocrites
- ❏ never really develop their own relationship with God

Now go back and circle one or two reasons that you've struggled with at one time or another (everyone does!).

What can you do to keep from dumping your relationship with God?

What's something you can do this week that will help you stay "plugged in" to God? When will you do it?

The one thing	When I'll do it

DANNY,
the Lion Tamer

Real Name:

Talk about the Lion King. **DANNY** stood up for what he believed. Well, it's probably more accurate to say he kneeled down for what he believed. The results were ferocious!

 Flashback

Read Daniel 6

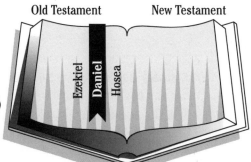

Old Testament   New Testament

Ezekiel   Daniel   Hosea

Check the correct answers:

1. Why did DANNY get in trouble?
   - ❏ He didn't do his homework
   - ❏ He prayed to God
   - ❏ He made a smart-mouth comment about the king
   - ❏ He refused to do his job

2. What was DANNY's punishment?
   - ❏ 40 lashes with a wet noodle
   - ❏ no TV for a week
   - ❏ thrown in jail
   - ❏ thrown in a lion's den

3. What was the result?
   - ❏ he died
   - ❏ everyone made him the new king
   - ❏ his actions had no impact
   - ❏ the king decided everyone should worship DANNY's God

Why do you think DANNY had the guts to do what he did?

FAST FORWARD

Give some advice to these students who are in DANNY-like situations:

Erin used to hang out with a pretty tough crowd until she moved to a new city and got active in her church youth group. The next summer Erin went back to visit her old friends. Every time they wanted to do something she knew was wrong, she'd tell them, "God wouldn't want me to do that. I'd better not." Her friends told her that if she didn't want to do stuff with them, she might as well go back home. What should she do? What should she say?

Phil makes extra money by walking his neighbor's dog every day after school. One day Phil had on a T-shirt that said "Jesus Christ is the Way" on it in really cool letters and colors. Old Man Thompson, the dog's owner, said to Phil, "Don't wear that shirt when you walk my dog . The neighbors will think I'm some weirdo religious fanatic." What should Phil do? What should Phil say?

Describe a situation in your own life right now where you could stand for God's truth, even though it might be really difficult:

What would it feel like for you to stand for truth?

SAM, the Mighty Man

Real Name:

OK, SAM was a major stud—probably the strongest guy in the whole Bible! But he had a mega-weakness too.

Read Judges 16:4-21

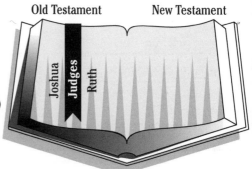

Old Testament   New Testament

Joshua   Judges   Ruth

Check the false explanations SAM gave Delilah for how she could break his great strength:

❏ hold kryptonite in his face
❏ tie him up with fresh thongs
❏ tie him up with new ropes

❏ tie him up with Australian goat hairs
❏ weave his hair into a fabric
❏ take away his protein drinks

Delilah nagged SAM until . . .

❏ he punched a hole in the wall
❏ he was tired to death

❏ he barked like a dog
❏ he married her

True or False:

T	F	SAM had the hots for Delilah.
T	F	Delilah wanted the best for SAM.
T	F	SAM made a bad choice by staying with Delilah.
T	F	SAM let his short-range desires ruin his long-range goals.

FAST FORWARD

If you could have $100,000 today or $1,000,000 in ten years, which would you take?

Why does sin often seem exciting even when the consequences are bad?

Here's a column of immediate things and a column of far-off things. For each pair, circle the one you'd choose (you can't choose both).

immediate	far-off
Buy a car when you're 17	Save the money for college
Take easy classes in high school	Take difficult classes in high school to prepare for college
Find the quickest way to get a job done	Find the best way to get a job done
Play another hour of video games and blow off your piano practice time	Practice your piano so you'll continue to improve
Buy this one totally hot CD right now	Save the money for your school ski trip next winter

Give an example of a decision like this you've had to make:

What did you do? Why?

If you could make that decision again, would you do it differently? Why or why not?

GiDDY,
the Frightened Wimp

Real Name:

GiDDY's terrified. His country is being attacked, and he's in hiding. But God has great plans for him, in spite of his fear.

 Flashback

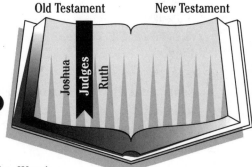

Old Testament   New Testament

Joshua Judges Ruth

Read Judges 6:11-17

● ● ● ● ● ● ● ● ●

When the angel of the Lord came to GIDDY, he addressed him as:

❏ Señor Guido   ❏ Mighty Warrior
❏ Chosen One   ❏ Captain Crunch

In this little wordsearch, find all the things people are afraid of (they're listed below). Put the remaining letters, in order, into the blanks below to spell out what we might call GIDDY.

Snake	Slime	God
New Stuff	Spiders	Stranger
Mice	Dogs	Dark
Bugs	Shark	Devil

S	S	C	A	B	U	G	S
N	E	W	S	T	U	F	F
A	R	E	L	D	O	G	S
K	S	P	I	D	E	R	S
E	D	Y	M	I	C	E	H
C	A	D	E	V	I	L	A
S	T	R	A	N	G	E	R
G	O	D	T	D	A	R	K

＿ ＿ ＿ ＿ ＿ ＿ ＿ ＿ ＿ ＿ ＿

＿ ＿ ＿ ＿ ＿

What was GIDDY afraid of (check out verse 15)?

FAST FORWARD

What were you afraid of as a little kid?

Rank these fears from 1 (scariest) to 10 (least scary):

____ speaking in front of my class
____ being asked about God
____ when my parents get angry
____ dying
____ violence
____ natural disasters (earthquakes, floods, tornadoes, etc.)
____ taking a test
____ telling someone you like him/her
____ doing something new
____ trying out for a team

What are you afraid of now?

How can God help you with that fear?

POOR MAMA,
the Giving Queen

Real Name:

It must have been pretty cool to be pointed out by Jesus as a positive example. **POOR MAMA** was singled out, not because she wore the best clothes to church or because she played an important role on the temple board. Jesus pointed her out because her heart was right.

 Flashback

Read Mark 12:41-44

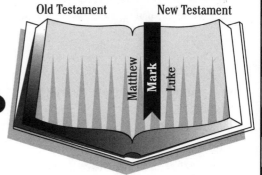

Old Testament   New Testament

Matthew Mark Luke

Why, exactly, did Jesus point out POOR MAMA?

Circle the picture that represents how much Poor Mama actually gave:

Circle the picture that represents the size of POOR MAMA's gift in God's eyes:

FAST FORWARD

Now circle the picture which represents your giving (of money) in God's eyes:

Answer one of these two questions:
- If you don't give any money or not much at all to God, why not?

- If you give a lot of money to God, why do you do it?

What other ways besides giving money can you "give" to God?

Give it up! Choose one form of giving you'll follow through on this week, then write when you'll give it:

❏ $	how much?	when & where?
❏ time/talent	what?	when & where?

SAMANTHA,
the Water Woman

Real Name: [   ]

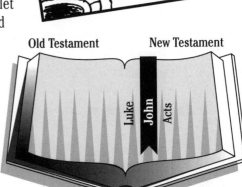

It's a little hard to get what's going on in this story unless you know what it was like to live back then. Jesus was a member of one race and **SAMANTHA** was a member of another. These two races were big-time enemies—they never talked, nor had anything to do with each other. So it was a major deal that Jesus would even talk to this lady, let alone offer her salvation! Jesus showed us that he would have nothing to do with racism.

Flashback
Read John 4:4-26, 39-42

● ● ● ● ● ● ● ●

Old Testament   New Testament

Luke John Acts

What race was SAMANTHA?

Samaritans are from:
- ❏ Samurai-ville
- ❏ Samaria
- ❏ Somalia
- ❏ the city where Sam and Mary got a tan

What race was Jesus?

If you picked up a copy of The Samaritan Enquirer *that ran a cover story about Jesus and SAMANTHA's encounter, what would the headline be?*

FAST FORWARD

Check examples of racism that you've seen recently:

- ❏ racist jokes
- ❏ graffiti
- ❏ racist remark aimed at another person
- ❏ discrimination (someone not getting picked for something because of his or her race)
- ❏ fighting as a result of race
- ❏ fear of another race

How do we become racist?

Why does God hate racism?

How can we get rid of racism in our own lives?

- ❏ smile and say hello to someone of another race
- ❏ stop telling racist jokes (or listening to them)
- ❏ invite someone from another race to your youth group
- ❏ ask God to take away your fears and prejudices

Now, add two more ideas:

- ❏ _____
- ❏ _____

ROOF CLUB,
Extra-Mile Friends

Real Names: unknown

Good friends are hard to come by—especially friends who will tear apart roofs for your benefit! What? Read on—these guys were *serious* about getting some help for their friend!

Flashback

Read Luke 5:17-26

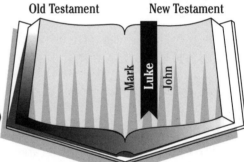

Old Testament   New Testament

Mark   Luke   John

● ● ● ● ● ● ● ●

Why couldn't the ROOF CLUB get into the house?

❏ they didn't have an invitation
❏ they weren't wearing proper attire
❏ the house was packed
❏ they were underage

How did the ROOF CLUB solve the problem?

❏ floated their friend in on a magic carpet
❏ lowered their friend down the chimney
❏ tossed their friend through the kitchen window
❏ removed roof tiles and lowered their friend on ropes

How did Jesus respond to their wild idea?

What reason does Jesus give for healing their friend?

FAST FORWARD

Describe a time you did a clear act of kindness for a friend:

If you were a friend of the following students, what radical act of friendship could you do for them?

Eric got his bike stolen yesterday. He's *totally* bummed because he uses it for his newspaper route, and now he has to walk.

Jessica just found out her grandmother died. Even though her grandmother lived on the other side of the country, Jessica really cared a lot for her.

Tony was out on his in-line skates when he tried a trick a bit too advanced for his ability. Now he has a cast on his leg and can't walk for two weeks.

What's a radical act of friendship you can do for someone this week?

Friend	Radical Act	When

REBOUND,
the Comeback Kid

Real Name:

REBOUND messed up royally! As a result, Paul wanted nothing to do with him. But later on we see the story has changed.

Flashback part 1

Read Acts 15:36-41

REBOUND is the guy Paul's not very excited about in this passage. In fact, Paul was pretty ticked, and wanted nothing more to do with REBOUND. Why?

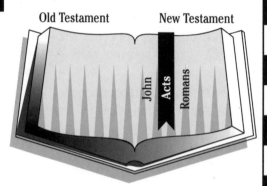

Old Testament   New Testament

John Acts Romans

REBOUND goes with Barnabas to:
- ❏ Cyprus
- ❏ jail
- ❏ the mall
- ❏ a disco

Flashback part 2

Read 2 Timothy 4:11

Some time has passed. What does Paul think of REBOUND now? Why?

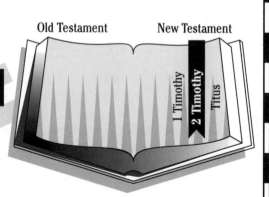

Old Testament   New Testament

1 Timothy 2 Timothy Titus

FAST FORWARD

Check the wrongs listed below that you've done:

- ❏ gossiped about a friend
- ❏ conveniently "forgot" my chores
- ❏ spent money when I shouldn't have
- ❏ accused someone of something he/she didn't do
- ❏ didn't try something I should have
- ❏ blew an important play in sports
- ❏ did sloppy work on an important school assignment
- ❏ ignored my alarm clock and overslept

- ❏ swore
- ❏ blew off my homework
- ❏ ate too much big-time
- ❏ made a prank phone call
- ❏ hurt someone's feelings
- ❏ broke something
- ❏ gave bad advice
- ❏ lost something important

Finish these sentences:

The dumbest wrong thing I've done this year is . . .

The last wrong thing I did was . . .

The best way to respond when I do something wrong is . . .

The best way to learn from doing wrong is. . .

Is there something you've done wrong in the last year that you can fix today?
- ❏ Yes
- ❏ No

If "yes," what can you do?

DAVE'S POSSE

Real Name: _____

Hold onto your socks—these are some of the coolest guys in the entire Bible! Their exploits are outrageous. They show us what can be done when we "go for it" with God!

Flashback

Read 2 Samuel 23:8-12, 18-23

Old Testament   New Testament

1 Samuel 2 Samuel 1 Kings

● ● ● ● ● ● ● ●

Match the POSSE members with their outrageous acts:

Josheb-Basshebeth   killed 300 men with his spear

Eleazar   hand froze to sword as he stood his ground and defeated an entire army

Shammah   killed 800 men with his spear in one fight

Abishai   fought a giant armed only with a club, and killed the giant with his own spear

Benaiah   defended a field of grain by himself

Put a star next to the POSSE member that you think did the most outrageous act.

If you were the 796th guy to go up against Josheb (he'd already killed the first 795), what would you do?

FAST FORWARD

I'm committed to carrying out outrageous acts for God this much:

```
/——————————/——————————/——————————/——————————/
0%          25%         50%         75%         100%
```

What kinds of outrageous acts for God could you do? (check all that apply.)

❏ stand up for truth in school
❏ share Christ with a friend
❏ be nice to someone who's not my friend
❏ ride a tricycle on the freeway
❏ give away some of my money to God's work

❏ bungee jump off a chair
❏ eat a can of cat food
❏ sit with a loner at lunch
❏ other:_____

"If I had more _____, I'd do more outrageous acts for God." (Choose one to fill in the blank.)

❏ faith
❏ confidence
❏ money
❏ other:_____

❏ time
❏ courage
❏ talents

Pick one outrageous act for God that you will try this week:

The one thing	When and where I'll try it

JAKE, the Stair Master

Real Name:

JAKE had really messed up (Genesis 27). He'd told a whopper of a lie to his dad in order to get something that rightfully belonged to his brother. This wasn't just a spur-of-the-moment lie. It was a fully-planned dramatic presentation! God was certainly not pleased with all of this. But look what happens soon after.

Flashback

Read Genesis 28:10-17

● ● ● ● ● ● ● ● ●

Old Testament   New Testament

Genesis Exodus Leviticus

Draw a picture of JAKE's dream:

God's love for JAKE was based on (check all that apply):
- ❏ his natural good looks
- ❏ his creative lying abilities
- ❏ his family name
- ❏ nothing—God just loved him
- ❏ all the good things he'd done
- ❏ the size of his offerings

FAST FORWARD

God's love for me is based on (check all that apply):

- ❏ my natural good looks
- ❏ my talents and abilities
- ❏ my Christian family
- ❏ nothing—God just loves me
- ❏ all the good things I do
- ❏ the size of my offerings

If God loves me just because he chooses to (not based on anything I do), that means (check all that apply):

- ❏ I should joyfully accept his love
- ❏ I might as well sin like crazy
- ❏ I don't have to live with a ton of guilt
- ❏ I should try to do right just because I love him
- ❏ I have to please him all the time or he'll stop loving me
- ❏ He must not be very smart
- ❏ There's nothing I can do to make him love me more
- ❏ There's nothing I can do to make him love me less

God loves you no matter what you do! What difference can this make in your life this week?

Big Daddy ABE

Real Name:

Adam was the father of humankind, but **ABE** was the father of the entire Jewish race. In fact, they didn't even exist before **ABE**. God made some incredibly cool promises to **ABE**.

 Flashback

Read Genesis 12:1-5

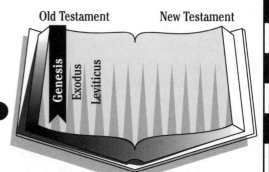

How old was ABE at this time?
- ❏ 2
- ❏ 14
- ❏ 75
- ❏ 143

Which of these things did God promise ABE (check all that apply)?
- ❏ ABE would always have good hair days.
- ❏ ABE would become a great nation.
- ❏ ABE's name would become great.
- ❏ ABE would be blessed.
- ❏ ABE would be able to sing like a bird.
- ❏ ABE would be the king.
- ❏ ABE would never die.
- ❏ God would bless those who were cool to ABE.
- ❏ The whole earth would be blessed through ABE.
- ❏ ABE was going to go to Disney World.

FAST FORWARD

Which of these things does God promise you? (Look for the answers at the bottom of this page.)

___ a. no zits, ever
___ b. answered prayer
___ c. victory over temptation
___ d. an easy life
___ e. tons of friends
___ f. guidance

___ g. life forever
___ h. megabucks
___ i. success in baking contests
___ j. forgiveness
___ k. you'll become babe-a-licious
___ l. great grades

Choose two of God's promises to you from the correct answers above and write what difference they can make in your life.

Finish this sentence:
The best thing about God's promises is . . .

(Here are the answers to the promises question: b, c, f, g, j.)

Almost **AGGIE**

Real Name:

AGGIE was the king, but he wasn't a Christian king. Paul wanted to do something about that fact. He spoke and, amazingly, **AGGIE** listened.

 Flashback

Read Acts 26:1-29

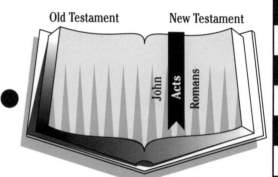

Old Testament   New Testament

John Acts Romans

AGGIE gave Paul permission to:
- ❏ sing an opera
- ❏ speak for himself
- ❏ roll over and play dead
- ❏ be excused to go to the bathroom

Paul's speech to AGGIE was about:
- ❏ what happened when he (Paul) met Jesus
- ❏ how to get grape juice stains out of cotton
- ❏ the best stores to buy carpeting
- ❏ why God loves AGGIE

How close do you think AGGIE came to responding to the truth of Christ?

/————————————/————————————/————————————/

1. not close at all   **2.** kind of close   **3.** very close   **4.** closer than stink on trash

Take a guess. Why do you think AGGIE didn't choose to follow Christ?

FAST FORWARD

Whom do you know who's kind of like AGGIE—this person has heard the truth, but has never really chosen it?

How do you respond when God points out something you need to do?

/—————————————————/———————————————————/

lousy　　　　　**sometimes good / sometimes bad**　　　　**great**

Check all the ways God has used to speak truth to you in the last year:

- ❏ the Bible
- ❏ a sermon at church
- ❏ my youth pastor
- ❏ Christian music
- ❏ prayer

- ❏ a friend
- ❏ the Holy Spirit just made it obvious
- ❏ my parents
- ❏ a hard lesson
- ❏ other: _____

You just told your friend how he or she can have a relationship with God. The response is, "Well, I don't know. I guess it makes sense—I just don't think it's for me." What would you say?

Bad Luck **BOiLS**

Real Name:

Once upon a time, **BOiLS** had it all—money, land, power, cool family. Then God allowed him to lose *all* of it! His friends gathered around and gave him a bunch of reasons why it all happened. But in the end, God himself speaks up and makes it pretty clear **BOILS** doesn't need to understand why—he just needs to trust God.

 Flashback

Read Job 38
(that's right—the whole thing!)

Old Testament   New Testament

Esther Job Psalms

● ● ● ● ● ● ● ● ●

God spoke to BOILS out of a:
- ❑ storm
- ❑ cereal box
- ❑ church
- ❑ burning bush
- ❑ tin can
- ❑ pay phone

In your own words, write out the question God asked BOILS that really grabbed you:

Why did God ask all these questions?
- ❑ to humiliate BOILS
- ❑ to help BOILS see he needs to trust God
- ❑ to show off
- ❑ to confuse BOILS

Pretend you're BOILS's friend, and you were there right before God started speaking. What advice would you give him?

FAST FORWARD

Is it OK to seek answers to things we don't understand?

❏ Yes   ❏ No

Why or why not?

If we can't find answers, what are we supposed to do?

List three things that don't seem "fair":

Write a prayer to God acknowledging that he's a lot smarter than you, and that you're willing to trust him no matter what things look like:

Dear God,

Love,

SHAD, SHAQ and ABE, the Firemen

Real Name: _____

This is a "hot" story! These three guys refused to give in and give up their beliefs, even though it meant certain bodily harm. The amazing thing is that the story gives us no indication that they ever even thought about giving in.

 Flashback

Read Daniel 3:8-30

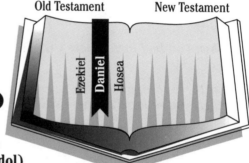

Old Testament   New Testament

Ezekiel Daniel Hosea

● ● ● ● ● ● ● ● ●

Circle the right words:

SHAD, SHAQ and ABE were working for **(Taco Bell, the king, a convenience store)**. A huge **(cake, truck, idol)** was built, and all the people of the land were commanded to **(sell apples, do a funny little dance, bow down to it)** every time the **(music, video game, tuba)** played. SHAD, SHAQ and ABE wouldn't do it because **(they would only worship God, they wanted to be troublemakers, they thought it was stupid)**. The king had them **(whipped, grounded, thrown into a massive fire)**. **(An angel, Abe Lincoln, Forrest Gump)** joined them in the fire and they were **(torched, a little singed, untouched by the fire)**. The king decided **(everyone should worship SHAD, SHAQ, and ABE; everyone should worship God; everyone should roast marshmallows)**.

What would you have been thinking if you were of the three, and about to get thrown in the fire?

FAST FORWARD

When you get in a fight with a friend, where's God?

When you get in trouble, where's God?

When you're afraid, where's God?

When you feel lost, where's God?

When you're lonely, where's God?

When things are going well, where's God?

What difference does it make that God is always with you?

Check all the things that can separate a Christian from God's love:*

- ❏ sin
- ❏ chewing with your mouth open
- ❏ ditching church
- ❏ failing to read the Bible

- ❏ nothing!
- ❏ getting a bad grade
- ❏ eating spicy food
- ❏ not praying

*Hint: See Romans 8:38-39.

JOE'S BROS,
the Sibling Sellers

Real Name:

Joe is one of the biggest heroes of the Old Testament. He lived for God. He had tons of wisdom, and he was a powerful leader. But in this passage, he kind of offended his brothers. He told them some dreams that made him sound pretty stuck-up.

 Flashback

Read Genesis 37:12-28

● ● ● ● ● ● ● ● ●

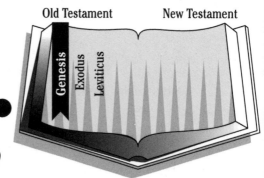

Old Testament   New Testament

Genesis   Exodus   Leviticus

What was JOE'S BROS' first plan? (see verse 18)

Reuben, one of the BROS, talked the rest into another plan. It was:
- ❏ tar and feather JOE
- ❏ tie JOE's shoelaces together
- ❏ throw JOE in a well
- ❏ give JOE a swirly

The final stage of their revenge was: (see verse 28)

If you were one of the brothers, what would you have said and done?

FAST FORWARD

Here are some possible reactions you might have when someone offends you. Rank them from best (1) to worst (10).

- ❏ get a gun and start blowin' people away
- ❏ take a moment to think before I react
- ❏ cry
- ❏ get revenge
- ❏ ignore the offense
- ❏ pout and stomp my feet
- ❏ ask God to help me forgive the offender
- ❏ calmly let the person know how he or she offended me
- ❏ carry a grudge for thirty-seven years
- ❏ walk away

Describe the last time someone offended you.

Describe your reaction—what did you do?

Is there another reaction that would have been better? If so, what?

A popular kid has been assigned as your partner for a history project. In front of the whole class, he says, "Oh, great! I get to work with the loser!" What do you do?

LUNCH BOY,
the Catutering King

Real Name: [_____]

This kid was in the right place at the right time—but he didn't even know it. No one, especially him, would have expected Jesus to use him that day. But, boy howdy, did Jesus ever use him!

 Flashback

Read John 6:1-15

● ● ● ● ● ● ● ● ●

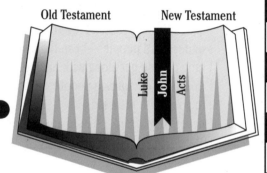

Old Testament   New Testament

Luke   John   Acts

True or False:

T   **F**   LUNCH BOY's mom packed him a lunch
T   **F**   LUNCH BOY knew Jesus had big plans for him
T   **F**   LUNCH BOY brought enough food for everyone
T   **F**   Jesus said, "I can use this boy's food because he has so much to give"
T   **F**   LUNCH BOY gave his little lunch to Jesus to use
T   **F**   LUNCH BOY was given a standing ovation for his wonderful actions

Write out LUNCH BOY's recipe for feeding five thousand people:

From the kitchen of: LUNCH BOY

Ingredients:

Instructions:

Feeds:_____

FAST FORWARD

Check all the abilities on the following list that you possess (even if it's a little):

- ❏ I listen well. People like to talk to me.
- ❏ I play a musical instrument.
- ❏ I'm friendly and make new friends easily.
- ❏ I'm somewhat athletic. I play one or more sports pretty well.
- ❏ I'm good with my hands and like to build things.
- ❏ I like computers. I can always figure things out on them.
- ❏ Fixing things is cool—I love doing it.
- ❏ I understand people—I can figure out their problems.
- ❏ I help people get along with each other.
- ❏ I'm able to encourage people with the things I say.
- ❏ I'm good with little kids.
- ❏ I'm very organized. I like to keep things orderly.
- ❏ Other:_____

Make up a story where God uses you and one of your abilities to do something really cool for him.

ABBiE,
the Hair-Care Specialist

Real Name:

ABBiE was blessed. Some people are blessed with riches, others with talent. **ABBiE** was blessed with hair. That's right—he had a head of hair that made women drool and made men jealous. But you might say **ABBiE** got a little too "caught up" in his hair!

Flashback

Read 2 Samuel 14:25-26, 18:9-17

● ● ● ● ● ● ● ●

Draw a picture of ABBIE while he was "involved" with the tree.

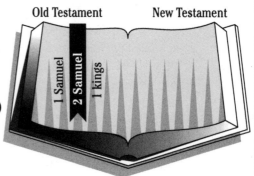

Old Testament   New Testament

1 Samuel   2 Samuel   1 kings

Circle the statements ABBIE probably would have said about himself:

"I'm so humble!"

"I'm such a stud!"

"Can't we all just get along?"

"I've got more hair in my nose than you'll ever have on your head."

"My desire in life is to be good person."

"I like hanging around in trees."

FAST FORWARD

What's vanity?

    a. a really small van

    b. a bathroom counter top

    c. an over-concern about how cool you are and how good you look

    d. a small ocean crustacean

What are some of the signs of a junior higher who has a lot of vanity? (By the way, the correct answer above was "c.")

Vain-O-Meter.
Draw a needle to show your level of vanity:

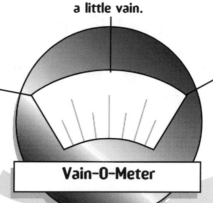

a little vain.

anti-vain. i'm so un-vain, i think i'm the scum of the earth.

mega-vain. i spend hours staring into a mirror.

Vain-O-Meter

ABBIE's vanity got him killed. Which three of these results of vanity could happen to you?

- ❏ lose friends
- ❏ draw my focus away from God
- ❏ cause me to neglect things that really matter
- ❏ cost me a lot of money
- ❏ make people think I'm stuck up
- ❏ harm my self-image once I get a reality check
- ❏ harm my future marriage

DAVE,
the Dancing Fool

Real Name: [   ]

Praising God can be a private thing. But sometimes it's a very public thing. **DAVE** had no reservations—he wanted to worship God, so he went for it. And public it was!

 Flashback

Read 2 Samuel 6:12-22

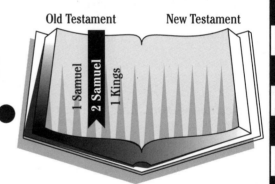

Old Testament   New Testament

1 Samuel   2 Samuel   1 Kings

● ● ● ● ● ● ● ● ●

How did DAVE praise God?

What would you have thought of DAVE if you'd been standing nearby watching?

Choose a title for this scene:
- ❏ Just Me and My Ephod
- ❏ Disco Dave's Dance-o-Rama
- ❏ Other:_____
- ❏ One Lord a-Leaping
- ❏ Dancing in the Streets

Why was Michal (DAVE's wife) so bothered by DAVE's act of worship (see verse 20)?

FAST FORWARD

When you're singing in church, how much do you care what people around you think of your singing?

/————————————/————————————/————————————/

1. Don't care at all—I sing my lungs out!

2. Don't care much—I rarely think about it.

3. I care—it makes me sing quieter than I might.

4. I care a lot! I just mouth the words!

Besides singing, how else can you praise God?

Write a short poem, praising God for some of his qualities (it can rhyme if you want, but it doesn't have to):

WHiNY BRO,
the Fair Share Demander

Real Name:

You read this story earlier in this book. But this time we're going to look at a different character. You may remember **PIG BOY**. Well, **WHiNY BRO** is **PIG BOY**'s older brother—and he needs a Happy Meal in a major way!

 Flashback

Read Luke 15:11-32

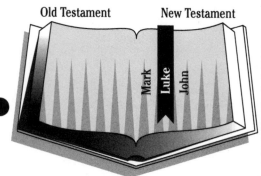

● ● ● ● ● ● ● ●

Match the brothers with their deeds
(each brother has three right answers):

PIG BOY

WHiNY BRO

hung out with prostitutes
never disobeyed
worked really hard
spent a bunch of money
got angry
hung out with pigs

What was WHINY BRO's complaint?
- ❑ "He gets to do everything."
- ❑ "My stomach hurts."
- ❑ "It isn't fair."
- ❑ "Turn down that loud music."
- ❑ "Someone ate all the nacho dip."

What was WHINY BRO's dad's response to his complaints?

FAST FORWARD

WHINY BRO was convinced it was his right to get certain things based on his actions. Some of what we might consider our rights are legitimate ("I have a right to breathe") and others are a bit more questionable ("I have a right to a Mercedes Benz"). What do you believe are some of your rights?

I believe it's my "right" to . . .

I believe it's my "right" to . . .

I believe it's my "right" to . . .

I believe it's my "right" to . . .

Now go back and rate your sentences—1 (easy to give up) to 4 (hard to give up).

What do you think God would say to you about your rights?

When could defending your rights cause you to sin like WHINY BRO?

RUTHiE,
the Displaced Widow

Real Name:

RUTHiE got a raw deal. First she marries this guy from another country and he takes her back there. Then the guy dies—and the guy's father too. So **RUTHiE** is left with her mother-in-law, whom she hardly knows at all, in a country that's not her own.

 Flashback

Read Ruth 1:3-18

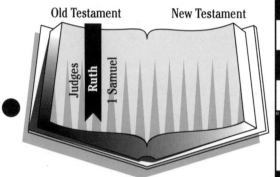

Old Testament   New Testament

Judges Ruth 1 Samuel

● ● ● ● ● ● ● ● ●

RUTHiE's sister-in-law was:
- ❏ Orca
- ❏ Oprah
- ❏ Orpah
- ❏ Oreo

RUTHiE's mother-in-law's name was:

RUTHiE had lots of options. If you were RUTHiE, which of the following options would you consider (check as many as you want)?

____ sit in a corner and pout
____ get an apartment on my own and make a new life for myself
____ find another husband, quick!
____ show loyalty to my new mother-in-law by staying with her
____ go back to my own country and leave my mother-in-law
____ go back to my own country and take my mother-in-law with me

Now go back and circle the option RUTHiE chose.

FAST FORWARD

What's loyalty? (circle one)

a. showing your allegiance or commitment to someone or something
b. being really proud of the accomplishments of a friend
c. when a boat turns upside-down
d. doing what you're supposed to do even when you don't feel like it

Whom are you loyal to? Why? (By the way, the answer to the question above is "a.")

Why does God care about loyalty?

❏ He never leaves me.
❏ He makes my life perfect.
❏ He always loves me.
❏ He gives me straight A's.
❏ He loves me more than he loves other people.

❏ He gave his Son for me.
❏ He offers me salvation.
❏ He forgives my sins.
❏ He allows me to live forever.

How does God show his loyalty to you?

Take a moment to pray, thanking God for his loyalty to you. Check here when you're done praying: ❏

PETE,
the Second-Chance Wonder

Real Name: _____

When you really blow it bad, there's nothing as sweet as forgiveness. **PETE** got to experience this in a major way.

Flashback part 1
Read Matthew 26:69-75

What did PETE do? Why?

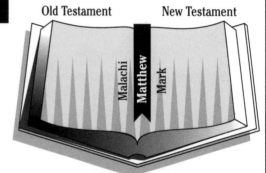

Old Testament   New Testament

Malachi | Matthew | Mark

What effect do you think this had on his relationship with Jesus?

Flashback part 2
Read Matthew 16:17-20

What are some of the things Jesus said about PETE?

Circle all the following phrases that are true.

PETE really blew it when he denied knowing Jesus

Jesus told PETE: "Now you can't be my friend—neener, neener, neener!"

Jesus changed his mind about PETE after PETE showed what a wimp he was

Jesus forgave PETE for denying him and still used PETE in the start-up of the church

FAST FORWARD

Whom do you have a hard time forgiving? Why?

What will it take for you to forgive this person?

How hard is it for you to believe God will forgive you when you mess up?

/————————/————————/————————/

not hard at all   **not too hard**   **kind of hard**   **impossible!**

Write a letter to God, asking for forgiveness for something:

I'm sorry, God . . .

Love,

JOSH & CAL,
the Scoutmasters

Real Name: [   ]

The people of Israel had been slaves in Egypt for a long time—and they finally got free. But they didn't go straight to the land that God had promised them. Instead, they roamed around the desert for a while. When they finally got to the Promised Land, they found out it was occupied—other people lived there. So Moses sent in spies to check it out. **JOSH & CAL** were two of the spies.

Flashback

Read Numbers 13:26—14:9

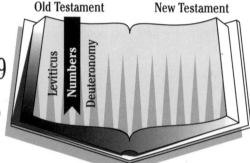

● ● ● ● ● ● ● ●

What tribes did the spies encounter?
(Check all that apply.)

❏ Hittites   ❏ Jebusites   ❏ Amorites
❏ Stalactites   ❏ Aerobic-tights   ❏ Summer-nights
❏ Canaanites   ❏ Amalekites   ❏ Go-fly-a-kites

What desert were the people wandering in?

❏ Sahara   ❏ Paran
❏ Mojave   ❏ Gobi

What was the land flowing with?

Why did the other spies think the people of Israel shouldn't go into the land?

Why did JOSH & CAL think they should go for it and take the land?

FAST FORWARD

What advice would you give to these students?

Raena's best friend has been bugging her about the two of them starting a prayer group at their school. Raena would like to go to a prayer group, but wishes someone else would start it.

Ben's friend Crystal is always reading horoscopes and telling him why she doesn't believe in God or heaven or hell. Ben wants to say something, but can't seem to get up the guts.

Michael plays on the select soccer team. His coach wants the team to practice every Saturday and Sunday morning. Michael wouldn't mind missing church once in a while, but every week seems like too much.

Describe something in your life like the problem the Israelites were facing—you know that God will give you the power to do this thing, but you're still afraid:

Give advice to yourself on the problem you just described:

When will you listen to your advice?

BARNEY,
the Friend Defender

Real Name:°

Paul (still known as Saul) just had his encounter with Jesus and became a Christian. Before that happened, he was one of the leading persecutors of Christians. He'd had them arrested by the dozens! So now that he's made this *major* change, the Jews he'd been working with *really* don't like him. And the Christians are still pretty nervous about him. One guy stuck up for him: **BARNEY**.

 Flashback

Read Acts 9:26-31

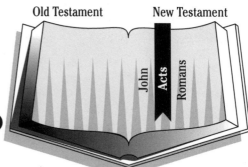

● ● ● ● ● ● ● ● ●

What did BARNEY do (check all that apply)?

❏ introduced Saul to the Christians
❏ showed Saul a cool juggling trick
❏ got Saul a great job as a waiter at the Jerusalem Country Club
❏ told the Christians Saul's story
❏ took a risk to reach out to a new friend

This is a Risk Meter. Draw a needle to show how much BARNEY risked by defending Saul (Paul):

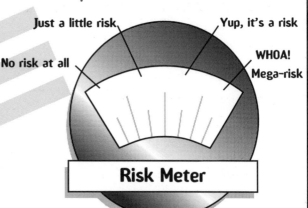

Just a little risk · Yup, it's a risk · No risk at all · WHOA! Mega-risk · **Risk Meter**

FAST FORWARD

Name someone from school who's not in your group of friends:

If this person wanted to become part of your group, but your friends were all suspicious, how big a risk would it be for you to stick up for the person?

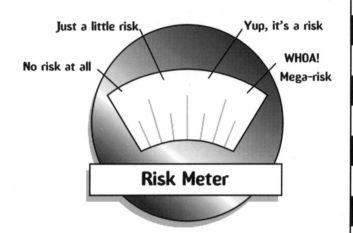

Just a little risk. Yup, it's a risk

No risk at all WHOA! Mega-risk

Risk Meter

Think really hard. Name one or two people who would probably like to be part of your group of friends.

What could you do to try to include him/her/them? When can you do this?

What I Can Do	For Whom	When

ZACK, the Tax Man

Real Name: [   ]

ZACK really wanted to see Jesus. One little problem (or maybe, one *short* problem): **ZACK** was a munchkin. In the crowd, all he could see were backs and shoulders!

 Flashback

Read Luke 19:1-10

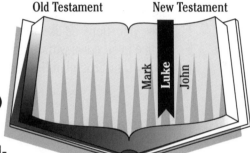

Old Testament   New Testament

Mark Luke John

● ● ● ● ● ● ● ● ● ●

Circle the correct words or phrases:
ZACK was sitting in a **(hydraulic lift, fig tree, second-floor window)** because Jesus was coming by and ZACK wanted to **(see him, ask him for some money, call him names)**. When Jesus was passing by, he looked up and **(shouted at ZACK, healed ZACK, saw ZACK)**. Jesus said, **("Look, a little wimp in a tree," "C'mon down, ZACK," "Why are you up there?")**. Then Jesus went **(to ZACK's house, to Jerusalem, to a coffee shop)** and **(ate, slept, watched TV)**.

Why was it a big deal that Jesus went to ZACK's house?

Which of these would have been your reaction if you were ZACK and Jesus said he was coming to your house for lunch?

❑ My room's a mess!
❑ Today would be a bad day
❑ WOW! You've got to be kidding!

❑ My house? Why?
❑ There's nothing good to eat at my house
❑ COOL! Let's go!

FAST FORWARD

True or False:

T   **F**   Jesus cares about my questions and problems.
T   **F**   There's stuff about me that keeps Jesus away.
T   **F**   I have questions I'd like Jesus to answer.
T   **F**   I'd like to sit down with Jesus and talk for a while.
T   **F**   I like sitting around in fig trees.

Just as ZACK climbed the tree, how can you seek Jesus?

What do you want to talk about with Jesus?

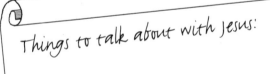

Things to talk about with Jesus:

HANNiE,
the Wannabe Nanny

Real Name: [_____]

Ooh! **HANNIE** wanted what she wanted really bad! She cried. She prayed. She cried some more. She prayed some more. Her husband even begged her to give up hope. In the end, she got her wish.

 Flashback

Read I Samuel 1:2-20

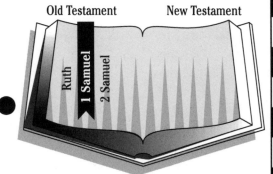

Old Testament   New Testament

Ruth
1 Samuel
2 Samuel

● ● ● ● ● ● ● ●

What did HANNIE want?

Why did the priest think she was drunk?
- ❏ she was dancing around the temple with a lamp shade on her head
- ❏ her lips were moving, but no sounds were coming out
- ❏ she fell down five times in the space of ten feet
- ❏ she failed her Breathalyzer™ test

What did HANNIE pray?

Why did she name her son Samuel? (verse 20)
- ❏ she liked the name
- ❏ because the priest told her to
- ❏ because she didn't name him Bob
- ❏ because she asked the Lord for him
- ❏ because Cindy was a girly name

FAST FORWARD

How does prayer work?

Why does God want us to pray?

If you pray for a million dollars, will you get it? Why or why not?

List 10 things you need to pray about:

1.   6.
2.   7.
3.   8.
4.   9.
5.   10.

Now take a few minutes and pray about at least three of them.

When else will you pray about them?*

Prayer Item	When I'll Pray
1. 2. 3.	

*Don't forget to DO iT!

ELi and the Flame Game

Real Name: [   ]

Usually, cutting yourself won't start a fire. It didn't this time either. Usually, dancing won't start a fire. It didn't this time either. Usually, a bunch of water *will* prevent a fire. It didn't this time.

Flashback

Read I Kings 18:20-40

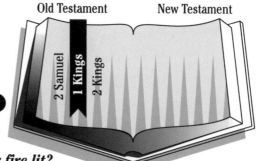

Old Testament   New Testament

2 Samuel 1 Kings 2 Kings

● ● ● ● ● ● ● ●

What did the priests of Baal do to try to get their fire lit?
(Check all that apply.)

- ❏ called Baal's name for hours
- ❏ danced around the altar
- ❏ called the Psychic Friends Network
- ❏ did kangaroo impersonations
- ❏ cut themselves with swords and spears
- ❏ ate Spam-burgers

What did ELI do that should've kept his fire from catching?

How did ELI's fire light?

Faith-Meter. Draw a needle that shows how much faith you think ELI had that God would light his fire:

some   lots

none at all   tons

Faith Meter

FAST FORWARD

What lesson can you learn from ELI's life? (Check all that apply).

- ❏ trust God to do the impossible
- ❏ call on God for all your barbecuing needs
- ❏ Baal's a loser
- ❏ God uses ordinary people to do amazing things

Think hard—write down five amazing things God could do through you.

1.

2.

3.

4.

5.

Pretend for a moment that God used you to do one of the amazing things you just wrote. What would it look like?

Spend a minute praying for courage to do this amazing thing, asking God to use you! Check here when you're done praying: ❏

Prayer List

date	prayer	date answered	answer

"TEN TO TWENTY"
(Say it ten times, fast.)

Okay, now take a break while we tell you what it means. 10 TO 20 produces events and products for students aged 10 to 20. Our writers, artists, producers and presenters are bound by a common passion: to present the Gospel to teenagers in the most effective, creative, powerful way possible. Here's how:

10 TO 20 EVENTS. Each year over 50,000 North American teenagers and youth leaders catch our high-involvement stage presentations at camps, conferences, concerts, schools, and youth rallies. Look for us in one of these programs (and if you're a youth leader sneaking a peek at this page, book us!)

live-media show
for junior highers

evangelism training
for high schoolers

live television for
teenagers

10 TO 20 PRESS. There are plenty of books you *have* to read. 10 TO 20 Press creates stuff you *want* to read. (We co-published this book.) Look for others titles, including *Cheap Thrills* and *Outrageous Dates*.

[OUR NAME IS THE AGE]

10 TO 20 · Box 604 · Del Mar, CA 92014 · 619 793-8275